SIX BRAVE PRESIDENTS

President Kennedy

SIX BRAVE

by Bill Davidson

Selects

PRESIDENTS

HARPER & ROW, PUBLISHERS
NEW YORK AND EVANSTON

* * * LONG BEFORE I ENTERED THE WHITE HOUSE I WAS DRAWN TO THE PROFILES OF EARLIER PRESIDENTS—THE PROBLEMS THAT CONFRONTED THEM, THE COURAGE THEY SHOWED, THE STANDARD THEY SET.

THEIR EXAMPLE IS EVEN MORE MEANINGFUL TO ME NOW—AS IT SHOULD BE TO ALL THE NATION. FOR THIS REASON I WAS GLAD THAT BILL DAVIDSON OFFERED TO SKETCH THESE STORIES OF DEDICATION TO THE NATIONAL INTEREST. RECALLING THIS NATION'S EARLIER TRIUMPHS OVER ADVERSITY GIVES US RENEWED HOPE IN ITS FUTURE.

PRESIDENT OF THE UNITED STATES

Contents

Preface   xi

Introduction: THE LAMP OF HISTORY   1

I   THE TALL MAN FROM VIRGINIA   6

II   DERISION FOR THE SCHOLAR   20

III   FROM HACK TO HERO   38

IV   THE DESPISED TAILOR   55

V   THE SPOILSMAN   70

VI   THE ROUGH RIDER   82

Epilogue: ILLUMINATION THROUGH THE WINDOW   94

Illustrations

GEORGE WASHINGTON 7

MARTHA CUSTIS WASHINGTON 11

WASHINGTON AND FAMILY AT MOUNT VERNON 12

WASHINGTON TAKING COMMAND OF THE ARMY 14

A PRESIDENTIAL RECEPTION IN 1789 18

JOHN QUINCY ADAMS AS A YOUNG MAN 21

THE HOME OF JOHN QUINCY ADAMS 23

JOHN Q. ADAMS' BALL FOR SENATOR ANDREW

    JACKSON 27

JOHN QUINCY ADAMS IN MIDDLE AGE 30

JOHN QUINCY ADAMS AS AN OLD MAN 35

ABRAHAM LINCOLN, 1865 39

LANTERN USED IN TORCHLIGHT CAMPAIGN PARADE 42

THE LINCOLN FAMILY IN 1861 45

CARTOON OF LINCOLN AND JEFFERSON DAVIS 50

LINCOLN TAKING THE OATH AT HIS SECOND
   INAUGURAL 53

ANDREW JOHNSON 56

JOHNSON TAKING THE OATH OF OFFICE 60

JOHNSON'S WHITE HOUSE OFFICE AND THE
   OVAL ROOM 65

CARTOON OF JOHNSON AS CAESAR 66

PRESIDENT JOHNSON AND THE CARPETBAGGERS 68

CHESTER A. ARTHUR 71

THE BIRTHPLACE OF CHESTER A. ARTHUR 73

ARTHUR TAKING THE OATH OF OFFICE 74

ARTHUR OUT-"SHINING" EVERYBODY IN
   HUMILIATION 78

CARICATURE OF CHESTER A. ARTHUR 80

THEODORE ROOSEVELT 83

ROOSEVELT AT AGES 4, 10–12, 18, 23 84

COLONEL ROOSEVELT OF THE ROUGH RIDERS 88

ROOSEVELT "BOWLING" AT GRAFT AND CORRUPTION 91

"WHEN THE PRESIDENT MAKES A SPEECH" 92

Preface

This book came about in a strange way, and therefore it has an unusual structure. It is built around six profiles of brave Presidents, which grew out of casual conversations I had with White House Press Secretary Pierre Salinger. These led to more formal discussions with Presidential Assistant Theodore C. Sorensen, and finally with President John F. Kennedy himself. The profiles appeared originally in a series of articles in THIS WEEK magazine.

The profiles are concerned primarily with the

specific period of each President's term of office in the White House. In this book, I have provided an introduction for each of them, describing each President's earlier life and picking up the threads of history which might explain more fully the acts of courage presented in the profiles themselves. The introductions are entirely my words and my ideas; the profiles into which they lead reflect the words and ideas of President Kennedy. Both introductions and profiles, however, have been read and approved by the President.

In addition to the cooperation of Mr. Salinger and Mr. Sorensen, I would like to acknowledge the technical help of Major Selma Herbert, U. S. Army (Ret.), and the research assistance of my daughter, Carol, a college student who well understands the importance of history.

Bill Davidson

1962

SIX BRAVE PRESIDENTS

Introduction
The Lamp of History

I have known President John F. Kennedy for some time now. Our friendship began when he was a brash young Congressman from Massachusetts and I was a brash young magazine writer from New Jersey. We played softball with the neighborhood kids near his home in Washington, while I interviewed him for the old magazine, *Collier's*. The article I wrote on Congressman Kennedy never was published, incidentally, because my editor said, "That boy will never get anywhere in politics."

That was in 1947 and we were both only twenty-nine years old, but even then I realized what a deep sense of history Mr. Kennedy had. As we drove around Washington together we'd stop at the statue of some Civil War general, such as General Philip Sheridan, and we'd talk of how Sheridan helped encircle General Robert E. Lee's Confederate forces in the last great battle of the Civil War. Or my companion would marvel at the beauty of the Jefferson Memorial as we passed it, and we'd discuss Thomas Jefferson's brilliance in buying the whole French province of Louisiana from Napoleon when actually it still was in the hands of Spain.

Later, when Mr. Kennedy was a Senator, I used to visit him in his office or on the floor of the Senate; it was obvious that his overwhelming interest in history had not diminished. Once, I walked with him from the Senate to the House of Representatives side of the Capitol, and it took us a half-hour to get through the Hall of Statues because he stopped to read the inscriptions on several of the statues of great Americans. Another time he led me into a little reception room off the Senate chamber to show me the table on which President Abraham Lincoln had signed the Emancipation Proclamation freeing the slaves.

After Mr. Kennedy became President and moved into the White House, he made a careful study of every nook and corner of the historic old mansion. He told me about a little room on the second floor which originally had been the sitting room of the wife of President James Monroe but which had been used as a secret meeting place by every President from Abraham Lincoln to Theodore Roosevelt. I was not surprised when it was announced, a few weeks later, that the room had been made over into a secluded conference room for President Kennedy.

The President not only has had this strong sense of history ever since he was a little boy but he has put his studies to good use and has become quite a world-famous historian himself. When he was barely out of his teen-age years, he wrote a book called *Why England Slept*, still considered one of the best written accounts of the crucial period leading to World War II. Then, in 1955, while he was recovering from a serious operation to correct a wartime injury to his back, he wrote *Profiles in Courage*, a book about famous United States Senators of past years who performed their duties in Congress with great bravery, often at the risk of their own political careers. This book won for the President the Pulitzer Prize for Biography, the first time any Chief Executive of the United States had been so honored for his literary efforts. As another great historian, Allan Nevins, wrote, "It should reassure Americans to know that their President understands so well the utility of the Lamp of the Past in guiding our feet."

It troubles the President, however, that so many American boys and girls do not strive to undertake a special study of history—the "Lamp of the Past" —so that they can comprehend the problems of the present and become good and useful citizens of our country. That is why he took time off from his busy schedule to sit down with me to discuss brave former Presidents, many of whom had sat in that same Oval Room office in the White House in which I was visiting him. He had come through a trying time of crisis in his first few months in office—Laos, Cuba, Berlin—but like many great leaders—Abraham Lincoln, Woodrow Wilson, Winston Churchill—his sense of urgency did not dim his appreciation of what we learn from history.

So, while the President's four-year-old daughter, Caroline, played outside the window with her dog, Charlie, and while Vice-President Lyndon Johnson came in from time to time with whispered news of a meeting of the National Security Council, the President and I talked about six outstanding examples of Presidential valor in the history of our country—those which have meant the most to him in his own period of lonely trial.

I

The Tall Man from Virginia

President Kennedy's first choice among the six brave Presidents is George Washington. Too many of us know only the hackneyed things about the Father of Our Country—his chopping down the cherry tree (probably untrue), his crossing of the Delaware River with his ragtag army to attack the Hessian mercenary troops in Trenton on Christmas Eve, his gracious family life at Mount Vernon. Many of us have little knowledge about the courage and strength which made him such a great man and such a great leader of our people.

6

Courtesy of The New-York Historical Society, New York City

GEORGE WASHINGTON, BY REMBRANDT PEALE

It is not even certain that we celebrate his birthday on the correct day. He was born on February 11, *not* February 22, according to the calendar then in use, in the year 1732. He was the son of Augustine Washington and the latter's second wife, Mary Ball, and he had four stepbrothers and stepsisters. He had very little formal education and experienced problems in both writing and speaking the English language until the day he died. His family was of average means—not extremely wealthy, as is commonly supposed—and there actually was not enough money to send George, the youngest of five children, to college. Instead, he was educated by private tutors, among them the Reverend James Marye, the Washingtons' pastor.

Another fallacy, spawned by the legend of George throwing a coin across the Potomac River, is that he was a fine athlete. Despite his unusual size (at six feet, three inches, he was one of the tallest men in Colonial America), he was not good at competitive sports. Moreover, he was shy and retiring; he had a badly pock-marked face, and he wrote about numerous "heartbreaks" in his relations with young ladies when he was a teen-ager. He did, however, have a good mind, with an almost fanatical attention to detail. When his eldest brother, Lawrence, died very young (as did all the other Washington children), George became the sole proprietor of the family's Mount Vernon estate. He was then only twenty, and he made it an extremely profitable plantation.

To give you some idea of his thinking as a young man, here are a set of rules which Washington made up to govern his own behavior, as he wrote them down at the age of fifteen:

1. Speak not of doleful things in a time of mirth.
2. When you see a crime punished . . . show pity to the suffering offender.
3. Utter not base or frivolous things among learned men.
4. Strive not with your superiors in argument.
5. Sleep not when others speak; sit not when others stand; speak not when you should hold your peace.
6. Let your recreations be manful, not sinful.
7. In visiting the sick, do not play the physician.
8. When a man does all he can, though it succeeds him not well, blame not him that did it.

9. Mock not or jest at anything of importance; break no jests that are sharp biting; and if you deliver anything witty or pleasant, abstain from laughing thereat yourself.
10. Labor to keep alive in your breast that little spark of celestial fire called conscience.

The celestial fire soon moved young George into public office. He became official surveyor of Culpeper County, Virginia, when he was seventeen, and when he was twenty-one, he was dispatched by Governor Robert Dinwiddie to see what a group of French intruders on Virginia soil were up to. The youth, returning from a difficult trip into the wilderness of western Virginia, reported that the French intended to invade English territory. He was then promptly appointed Lieutenant Colonel of the Virginia militia, and when the Colonel died, he assumed command. Barely out of his teens, he led his troops bravely in the disastrous British expedition against Fort Duquesne in the French and Indian War. Four times bullets pierced his coat, and two horses were shot out from under him. For his valor, he was elected to the Virginia House of Burgesses, but most of the time

MARTHA CUSTIS WASHINGTON, BY REMBRANDT PEALE

From a painting by Chappel

WASHINGTON AND FAMILY AT MOUNT VERNON

the shy young man merely sat in the parliament in embarrassed silence. One day the Speaker of the House had to come to Washington's rescue by saying, "Your modesty is equal to your valor. And both are beyond words."

In 1759, Washington met, wooed, and won the hand of Mrs. Martha Custis, a young widow with two small children. After their marriage, they returned to his estate at Mount Vernon, where he continued his success as a farmer. He also became a magnificent horseman, a skilled carpenter, and a competent blacksmith. He was living the peaceful life of a country gentleman when the War for Independence against England broke out. John Adams, remembering Washington's military brilliance in the French and Indian War, recommended him to be Commander in Chief of the Revolutionary Army. The "celestial fire of conscience" flared up in Washington again and he gave up his life of luxury to take command of the Continental troops besieging Boston, on July 3, 1775.

That was the beginning of six years of incredible

From a painting by Chappel

WASHINGTON TAKING COMMAND OF THE ARMY, 1775

frustration and hardship for the big, shy man from Virginia. Although some history books might lead you to believe that he led the American Army in glorious orthodox combat against the British, such was not the case. He never had more than 20,000 men in his command, and at times the number dwindled to less than 2,000. Opposing his motley group of sixty-year-old farmers and sixteen-year-old schoolboys were some 40,000 superbly trained British and Hessian soldiers. Until the very end of the war, when he received strong reinforcements from France and other foreign countries, he rarely could afford to meet the enemy in head-on combat. Instead, he conducted what would be known today as guerrilla warfare. His tactics featured hit-and-run raids, stealth and guile. Before the Battle of Princeton, he built campfires for about a mile along the rim of a hill, so that the enemy might think the Americans were camping there for the night. But Washington quietly withdrew and marched around the other side and defeated a large British detachment at dawn. On the outskirts of Brooklyn, he painted rows of black dots on canvas in such a way that, from the city, they looked like rows of cannon mouths. When the British saw what they imagined to be batteries of artillery, they beat a retreat. At one point during the war, Washington, with no gunpowder, maintained a post within musket-range of twenty British regiments.

So Washington's courage as a general is undoubted, but President Kennedy admires him even more for the courage he displayed when, eight years later, he became the first President of the United States.

Profile Number 1

WASHINGTON PULLS A NEW NATION TOGETHER

When George Washington was inaugurated as first President of the United States on April 30, 1789, he stepped directly into a morass of troubles. He was so low in funds personally that he had to borrow 600 pounds from a friend in order to move to New York from Virginia to take over the reins of government. The government's paper money had depreciated to zero in value, and the new nation's financial state was in such chaos that the easiest way to send money from New York to Philadelphia was via a bank in London.

No taxes were being collected, and the Union itself was in a condition of near anarchy. Vermont was declaring itself an independent country; tiny Rhode Island regarded itself as *the* United States— New York, Virginia, and all the rest playing the part of illegal seceders—stating that the Constitution would *never* be ratified in Providence; North Carolina, too, had not yet joined the Union.

It was a mess. Nevertheless, with the courage, perseverance, persuasiveness, and executive ability that he had exhibited as Commander in Chief of the American forces in the Revolution, Washington proceeded to build his new country from the bottom up.

By the end of his first year in office, he had won Vermont, Rhode Island, and North Carolina away from their position of recalcitrance. He had also laid to rest widespread fears of tyranny by

A PRESIDENTIAL RECEPTION IN 1789

pushing the Bill of Rights through the Congress.

He had assembled a brilliant working Cabinet in Thomas Jefferson, Alexander Hamilton, Henry Knox, and Edmund Randolph; the new Government began to levy taxes and establish a sound currency; a new civil service, far different from the corrupt systems of Europe, was created; and an efficient Federal Judiciary, with John Jay as Chief Justice, was appointed.

In a matter of months, Washington not only had welded the squabbling ex-colonies into a struggling but cohesive nation, but had established his own place in history as one of the greatest Chief Executives this country has ever had.

II

Derision for the Scholar

It is not surprising that the second of President Kennedy's six brave Presidents is John Quincy Adams. Mr. Kennedy has always looked up to this little-known President from his own state of Massachusetts as a model of honesty, integrity, and valor in government. He devoted a long chapter in his *Profiles in Courage* to John Quincy Adams' brave fight, as a United States Senator, to maintain his own standards of decency, as opposed to the selfish desires of his party. In his discussions with me, President Kennedy made it

JOHN QUINCY ADAMS AS A YOUNG MAN

clear that this strange and lonely man fought an equally courageous battle as President of the United States.

Your history teachers may have devoted little time to John Quincy Adams, except to note, perhaps, that he was the son of John Adams, our second President and one of the great architects of the Declaration of Independence and the Constitution. The younger Adams was a colorless man —short, bald, and scholarly—and he has been completely submerged in history by the more flamboyant politicians of his day, such as Andrew Jackson, Henry Clay, John C. Calhoun, and Daniel Webster.

He was born in Braintree, Massachusetts, in 1767. When he was eleven years old he went to Paris, where his father had been sent on a diplomatic mission to the French government during our Revolution. From then on, until he reached young manhood, he remained in Europe, receiving a fine education in Paris, Amsterdam, and at the University of Leyden in the Netherlands. At the age of fourteen, he became a private secretary

Wood engraving from *The Family Magazine*, 1840

Courtesy Library of Congress

THE HOME OF JOHN QUINCY ADAMS, QUINCY, MASSACHUSETTS

to Francis Dana, our envoy to Russia, and he traveled with him through Germany and to St. Petersburg, the capital of the Czars. After that, he wandered around Europe until he was eighteen years old, studying architecture and painting and enjoying discussions with such famous American revolutionaries as Benjamin Franklin and Thomas Jefferson. Finally, his father insisted that he return to the United States to complete his studies at Harvard College and study law. Young Adams complied with his father's wishes, but much against his will. He wrote letters to friends indicating that he would have preferred to remain in Europe living as a sort of eighteenth-century bohemian.

He graduated from Harvard in 1787, the year our Constitution was written, and then became a law student in the office of Theophilus Parsons in Newburyport, Massachusetts. He was admitted to practice in 1790, when he was twenty-three, and he soon set up his own law office in Boston. He was not a very successful lawyer. Like our own President Kennedy, his first love was writing, and he spent most of his time publishing articles, under a variety of pseudonyms, discussing the knotty problem of whether or not the infant United States should observe neutrality in Europe's many wars. During this period, as throughout the rest of his life, he was completely dissatisfied with himself—a trade mark of many other great men. He wrote to a friend, "I still find myself as obscure, as unknown to the world, as the most indolent or the most stupid of human beings."

By 1794, however, his brilliant articles on foreign affairs had attracted such widespread attention that President George Washington selected him as our Minister to Holland, though Adams was then only twenty-seven. Three years later he settled down to a long, happy marriage with Louisa Catherine Johnson, the daughter of the American consul in London. From then on his career blossomed until he became almost as famous as his illustrious father. He continued to write, and his articles on the political thinking of James Madison and James Monroe were regarded as masterpieces of their day. In politics, he became an envoy to

England, the Minister to the kingdom of Prussia, a State Senator, and finally, in 1803, United States Senator from Massachusetts.

Adams was thirty-six when he entered the Senate. One of his first acts on the floor of that august body caused a storm of controversy. The Federalist Party, which his father had helped to found and which had selected him for the Senate seat, was bitterly opposed to the Louisiana Purchase by President Thomas Jefferson. With characteristic independence, however, young Adams voted for an $11,000,000 appropriation to enable Jefferson to buy from Napoleon the vast area west of the Mississippi River. He was the only member of the French-hating Federalist Party in the Senate to do so. His reason? He felt that westward expansion was essential for the United States as a whole, and he was not concerned with the Federalists' almost fanatical desire to maintain New England as the richest and most important segment of a compact America which they could continue to control financially. "Curse on the stripling!" wrote a prominent Federalist, after labeling Adams' vote "an act of perfidy."

SCENE AT A BALL GIVEN BY JOHN Q. ADAMS FOR SENATOR
ANDREW JACKSON DURING THE MONROE ADMINISTRATION

This was the beginning of a four-year period during which Adams became what amounted to a one-man minority in the Senate. He was considered "cold, tactless and rigidly conscientious." He voted against his party on the most routine motions when he thought something dishonest was contemplated, such as a resolution for the Senate to go into executive session to give the appearance in the record of doing business when actually there was none to be done. He was completely nonpartisan, and he supported or rejected each issue solely according to the dictates of his own conscience. He spoke of members of his own party as people "who hate me rather more than they love any principle."

The final break between Adams and his party came when he was still a freshman Senator, in his fourth year in Congress. The British Navy, then engaged in a war with the French, began stopping American ships and seizing any American sailor for service in the King's Navy if he had been born on British soil—and, at that early period in our history, many of them were so born. Proof of American citizenship was not accepted.

The two major American political parties split on this issue. The Democratic-Republican party, headed by President Thomas Jefferson, became patriotically indignant and called for retaliatory action against the British. The Federalists, basically pro-British and anxious to preserve New England shipping even at the cost of appeasement, were against any action that might provoke the seizure or destruction of American vessels. In this conflict of opinion, Federalist Adams not only sided with the Republicans but led the attack in the Senate with a series of resolutions calling for a limit on British imports into the United States, as well as other drastic measures.

When the British warship *Leopard* fired on the American frigate *Chesapeake* just off the Virginia Capes, after the *Chesapeake* had refused to hand over four seamen whom the British claimed were British subjects, it was John Quincy Adams who led the fight in Congress for an embargo which prevented all British ships from entering American waters. The embargo went into effect, and New England was plunged into a depression. Its ship-building industry came to a standstill, its British-

JOHN QUINCY ADAMS IN MIDDLE AGE

based commerce stopped, and its farmers were unable to export a good portion of their products. Throughout strongly Federalist New England, Adams was denounced as "a scavenger," "a traitor," and worse. His only support came from his aged father who declared that his son's course was the obvious and honorable one. But even this was to no avail. John Quincy Adams was read out of the party when the Federalist-controlled Massachusetts legislature met in special session, with the express purpose of electing his successor—some nine months before his term was to expire. Adams then felt there was only one honorable course open to him. He resigned his Senate seat.

Such an overwhelming defeat would have killed off the career of a lesser man, but John Quincy Adams went on to become a superb Secretary of State under President James Monroe. It was he who formulated the principle of the Monroe Doctrine. His over-all statesmanship and devotion to duty was such that in the election of 1824—even with no party to back him—he emerged as one of the leading candidates for the Presidency. He took his record of honesty, valor, and recurrent defeat into the White House with him and thus became one of President Kennedy's six brave Presidents— more than a century after the political experts of his day predicted that he would quickly be forgotten.

Profile Number 2

JOHN QUINCY ADAMS REFUSES TO BACK DOWN

John Quincy Adams is not ordinarily thought of as one of the great Presidents; yet no man exhibited greater courage—in the face of tremendous obstacles—than he did in the first few months of his administration.

He came into office under a cloud. In the election of 1824, he had run second to a popular war hero, Andrew Jackson. Still, with Henry Clay and William H. Crawford also in the race, none of the candidates had a majority in the Electoral College.

This threw the election into the House of Representatives, where the Constitution specifies each state has only one vote in such proceedings. There, in a dramatic move, Clay asked his supporters to vote for Adams, and the outraged Jackson group saw their man beaten by the bald, rotund, colorless son of ex-President John Adams. Their outrage was compounded when Adams then named Clay his Secretary of State on the grounds that he was the most qualified man for the job. The Jackson people shouted "Corrupt Bargain," and Adams took office on March 4, 1825, in a state of open warfare with a bitter, turbulent, powerful faction in Congress.

From the very beginning of his term, Adams was vilified on the floor of the Senate in language that no other President has been subjected to. Senator John Randolph of Virginia denounced the Adams-Clay duo as "the combination of the Puritan with the blackleg (crooked gambler) . . . between old Massachusetts and young Kentucky —not so young, however, as not to make a prudent match and sell her charms for their full value."

When Adams proposed to his rebellious Congress that he was going to send American delegates to a Congress of the American Nations (who had just successfully revolted against Spain), there were more insults and outcries against the United States getting involved with ex-slaves who had overthrown their masters and with such new nations as the Negro Republic of Haiti. Again, Randolph led the diatribe and, as President Kennedy told me, "in what is perhaps the most memorable and malignant sentence in the history of personal abuse, Randolph denounced the aged mother of Secretary of State Clay for bringing into the world 'this being, so brilliant yet so corrupt, which, like a rotten mackerel by moonlight, shines and stinks.' "

After this attack on himself and the President, Clay challenged Randolph to a duel and scored what should have been a mortal wound. Randolph, however, had wrapped yards of flannel around his body beneath his coat and the shot only pierced the flannel.

In the face of such opposition—which, says

JOHN QUINCY ADAMS AS AN OLD MAN

President Kennedy, "makes my problems with Congress pale into insignificance"—Adams persevered. He was friendless; he had no party behind him, and he steadfastly refused to give out federal jobs as patronage. His theory was to strengthen the Federal Government beyond the dreams of Alexander Hamilton, and he continued to appoint men because of their ability and not their party affiliation. He wanted to build roads and canals to unite the country so it would not fly apart in sectional civil wars. But his administration ended after one term as it began—in total frustration.

In defeat, however, John Quincy Adams showed more courage than other Presidents have in victory. When Andrew Jackson defeated him for reelection in 1828, Adams ran for Congress and represented his Massachusetts district in the House of Representatives for nearly twenty years.

In the House he fought for all the ideals he had espoused during the heartbreak years as President, and he won victories against patronage and for roads, education, science, a naval academy and a strong Federal Government. He became one of the nation's most fiery opponents of slave power. He collapsed and died in Congress, still fighting, at eighty.

President Kennedy says, "I salute John Quincy Adams as one of the most courageous of our Presidents because he knew that he had lost the campaign of 1828 in the first few months of his administration in 1825 when he refused to make political appointments. But he never once backed down from his ideals."

III

From Hack to Hero

The third of President Kennedy's six brave Presidents is a man who would have to be included on any such list—Abraham Lincoln. I do not think, however, that Mr. Kennedy admires Lincoln for the usual reasons that have been emphasized in the schools. The great Civil War President is often cited as the perfect example of the Horatio Alger rags-to-riches hero, having risen to the White House from extremely humble beginnings in a Kentucky log cabin. Mr. Kennedy's admiration stems from deeper roots—a re-

oto by Gardner, April 9, 1865

ABRAHAM LINCOLN, 1865

spect for a man of seemingly limited ability who, under the stress of a catastrophe that was not of his making, rose to magnificent heights of courage and executive brilliance.

If the United States had not been ripped apart by the tragic issue of slavery, it is conceivable that Abraham Lincoln would have lived out his days in obscurity as a prosperous but undistinguished small-town lawyer, dabbling only in local political issues, such as whether or not the Sangamon River in Illinois should be dredged. He was born into a family of nondescript ancestry, except for possible descent from a Virginia aristocrat through his maternal grandmother. His father, Thomas, was a drifter and squatter. He floated from one wilderness community to another, built a log cabin, raised a crop, and then moved on.

The stories about Lincoln's struggles to educate himself when he was a boy are true. The stories about Lincoln, the rural wit, and Lincoln, the honest storekeeper, are likewise true. What is often overlooked is the fact that after Lincoln pulled himself up to a certain level of intellectual and

economic advancement, he remained there, without further progress, for many years. In the meantime, he had thought seriously of learning the
blacksmith trade instead of studying law, and at
various times he was a private in the Army, a vil-
lage postmaster, and a surveyor. His career easily
could have been in any of these areas and he would
have remained lost to history. He liked politics,
however, and after an unsuccessful attempt to get
elected to the Illinois state legislature in 1832, he
finally made it in 1834. This gave him the will to
continue with his study of the law, and he was able
to begin practice in Springfield, Illinois, in 1837,
when he was twenty-eight. He was a good lawyer
and prospered, and five years after he opened his
law office, he married Mary Todd, the sister-in-
law of Governor Ninian W. Edwards of Illinois.

The six-foot-four-inch Lincoln was a big,
homely man of changing moods, who, according
to historian Carl Sandburg, could shift from rol-
licking, droll storytelling to periods of deep gloom
in which "he lapsed silent and solemn beyond any
bystander to penetrate." He served four terms in

Courtesy of The New-York Historical Society, New York City

LANTERN USED IN A TORCHLIGHT CAMPAIGN PARADE

the state legislature, during which he alternately
amused his colleagues with his wit and pained them
with his depressions. Aside from that, his early
career as a politician was completely undistinguished. He was, in the legislature, what would be
known today as a "party hack." He was a member
of the Whig Party, the political descendants of the
old conservative Federalists, and he voted the
straight party line on nearly every issue. He
proposed no outstanding legislation and seemed
content merely to do political favors for his constituents. He paid very little attention to the
burning issue of the day, slavery, and avoided any
contact with the abolitionists, whom he considered
to be dangerous radicals. He felt that slavery was
wrong and an injustice, but in those early days he
did little or nothing about it. The same was true in
the period from 1846 to 1848, when he served one
term in Congress. He told his amusing backwoods
stories to his fellow Congressmen and devoted
most of his time to routine petitions and appointments and pensions for his constituents. By now,
however, the national issues were becoming so
overwhelming that this was not enough for the

people. He infuriated them with what seemed like a double standard by voting censure of President James Polk for the Mexican War, while at the same time voting for supplies and aid for the soldiers. His constituents did not return him to Congress for a second term in the elections of 1848.

The truth of the matter is that during his uninspired years, from 1834 to 1856, Lincoln was a very good lawyer and orator, but a distinctly second-rate politician. For five years after his flop as a Congressman, he wasn't even in politics at all. He devoted himself to his law practice and became a comparatively wealthy man, as his firm grew to the point where it was handling more than a third of all the cases that were heard in the Sangamon County Circuit Court in Illinois.

It wasn't until 1854, when he was forty-five, that Lincoln began to shake off the torpor that seemed to have gripped him for two decades. He finally was stirred by the issue of whether or not slavery should be permitted in the territories of Kansas and Nebraska; and when antislavery Whigs left their party to form the new Republican Party with dissident Democrats and Independents, Lin-

THE LINCOLN FAMILY IN 1861
l. to r., Mary, William Wallace, Robert Todd, Thomas, the President

coln went with them. He ran for United States Senator in 1854 and lost, and in 1856 he became the unsuccessful Republican Party nominee for Vice-President of the United States, with General John C. Frémont as the Presidential candidate. Then came a second campaign for the Senate in 1858. This was the famous one in which he debated Stephen A. Douglas all over the state of Illinois. Though he lost again, the debates were covered by newspapers from as far away as New York, and the people of the North began to be stirred by his homespun personality and his skillfully delivered words. In one brilliant speech he said, "A house divided against itself cannot stand. I believe this government cannot endure permanently half-slave and half-free. . . ." And the idea became one of the cornerstones of the antislavery movement. However, Lincoln himself remained a moderate on the problem of slavery. He was concerned with the human rights involved, but he was more concerned with the disastrous split in American unity which the institution of slavery was causing.

By 1859, Lincoln's oratory had made him a

national figure, and his law practice in Springfield
was all but forgotten. He was invited to speak at
Republican rallies throughout the Midwest, and
soon there were strong demands for him to come
to New York City, where he addressed thousands
of people at Cooper Union. This was followed by
a triumphal speaking tour of New England, the
hotbed of abolitionist sentiment. By the end of this
tour, it was a foregone conclusion that the former
small-town Illinois political hack—thrice defeated
for major national office—was a leading candidate
for the Presidential nomination of the new Republican Party. At the party's convention in Chicago
in May, 1860, Abraham Lincoln was nominated
on the third ballot.

But he still might have remained in historical
obscurity had it not been for another fortuitous
occurrence. In the six-month period before the
election, the dominant Democratic Party—torn
internally by the dissension of the more rabid par-
tisans of slavery—fragmented into three parts.
Thus Lincoln was opposed not only by the regular
Democratic candidate, Stephen A. Douglas, but

also by two Southern Democratic dissidents, John
C. Breckenridge of Kentucky and John Bell of
Tennessee. Lincoln received 1,866,452 votes,
Douglas 1,376,957, Breckenridge 849,781, and
Bell 588,879. Together, the three Democrats had
a million more votes than Lincoln. With a little
more than one-third of the total vote, he was dis-
tinctly a minority President.

On February 11, 1860, Lincoln left Illinois
with his family on the long journey to Washington. His trip was made chaotic by rumors that an
assassin was waiting for him on the train between
Philadelphia and Baltimore. Lincoln made a detour
and arrived in Washington unheralded and unwel-
comed, to take up his almost impossible job of
being President.

Profile Number 3

ABRAHAM LINCOLN
SAVES THE UNION

No man embarked on a more turbulent sea of

troubles when he became President than Abraham Lincoln. On the day he took office—March 4, 1861—he already faced a divided nation on the brink of fratricidal war.

South Carolina had seceded shortly after he had been elected in the preceding November, and Georgia, Alabama, Florida, Mississippi, Louisiana, and Texas quickly followed their sister state out of the Union. Arkansas, Virginia, North Carolina, and Tennessee were on the verge of secession. A month before Lincoln's inauguration, the Confederate States of America had been formed.

The United States Army numbered only 17,000 and the Navy's forty wooden ships were scattered over the seven seas. The seceded states had already occupied all Army and Navy bases in their territory and only two—Fort Pickens in Pensacola, Florida, and Fort Sumter in Charleston, South Carolina—were holding out. The first decision Lincoln had to make when he took office was whether or not to provision the Fort Sumter garrison, whose food supplies were dwindling. The South had made it clear that they would consider such an attempt to

THAT DRAFT

Jeff Davis: "Shut that door, Slidell Alexander! That Draft from the North will be the death of me—I *feel* it!"

Slidell Alexander: "C-c-can't shut it, Massa. Abe Lincoln's *got his back 'gainst it.* Better try a little o' dis de doctor left ver"

be an act of war. ("I hope I never have to make such a decision," Mr. Kennedy told me.)

The newly elected President waited a month before he took any action, because he wanted to exhaust every possibility of keeping Virginia, the richest and most powerful of the Southern states, and with strong anti-secessionist sentiment, in the Union. He took a calculated risk in so doing because, in the interim, many of the best officers in the Army went over to the Confederacy. Also, Lincoln had to fight off harebrained schemes in his own cabinet, one of which, proposed by Secretary of State Seward, urged that the President deliberately pick a fight with the world's great powers, France, Spain, England, and Russia, in order to reunite the North and South in a war of conquest. In the extraordinary document in which he proposed this plan, Seward also suggested that Lincoln appoint him his prime minister to execute the policy. Lincoln politely rejected the Seward plan.

Finally, at the beginning of April, Lincoln could see but one course open to him. He dispatched an expedition of relief ships to attempt to rescue the

Fort Sumter garrison, headed by Major Robert Anderson. The President realized that this would cause the Confederate batteries to open fire, but he felt there was no other honorable decision he could make.

At four-thirty on the morning of April 12, 1861, when Anderson refused to surrender and evacuate the fort, the Confederate batteries fired the first shots of the War Between the States. By nine o'clock the next morning, Fort Sumter's barracks were reduced to flame and ashes, the battlements and fortifications were crumbling, and the American flag had been shot away. Early that afternoon, Major Anderson surrendered.

In Washington, Abraham Lincoln set about making the initial decisions of his administration, decisions which eventually were to win the war. He decided on a policy of blockade and strangulation of the Confederacy. From the group of untried generals available to him he presently chose the thirty-four-year-old George B. McClellan, who, though he was stubborn and recalcitrant and won no brilliant victories, whipped the amateur-

Harper's Weekly Yearbook, 1865

LINCOLN TAKING THE OATH AT HIS SECOND INAUGURAL, MARCH 4, 1865

ish Army of the Potomac into a skilled fighting force.

When the President was urged to discipline McClellan after the General had insulted him, Lincoln said, "I will hold McClellan's horse if he will only bring us success."

In those first few months of his administration, Lincoln suffered many other insults, taunts, and setbacks. He was sniped at by his own party, impeded by the apathy of powerful interests, embarrassed by the excessive zeal of some of his more rabid supporters.

Through all those crisis-ridden months and years, Lincoln held steadfastly to one great goal—preservation of the Union. And the Union was preserved.

IV

The Despised Tailor

When President Kennedy selected his six brave Presidents for me, I reacted with surprise and curiosity to his fourth and fifth choices—as I think many other Americans will. The subject of the President's fourth profile in Presidential courage is Andrew Johnson, who assumed office after the assassination of Abraham Lincoln, and who generally is treated with a few offhand pages in the history books.

Andrew Johnson's life story is one of boyhood hardships, adult insecurities, and almost constant

PORTRAIT OF ANDREW JOHNSON

ridicule from his friends as well as his enemies. One biographer, Frank Moore, referred to him as "illiterate, ill-mannered, intemperate, stubborn, intolerant, quarrelsome, honest and well-meaning, but a fool." With all the ridicule, however, even his enemies admired his rugged honesty, his great native force of intellect and exceeding strength of will, his love for the Union and his genuine patriotism.

He was the only tailor ever to inhabit the White House. Tailoring was his trade long after he had entered politics, until the time he left his home in Tennessee to go to Washington as a Congressman when he was forty-five.

Like Lincoln, he came from the humblest of backgrounds. He was born in Raleigh, North Carolina, in 1808. His father, Jacob Johnson, was a porter whose job was sweeping and cleaning a Raleigh bank, and young Andrew was apprenticed out to a tailor when he was only ten. His education was fragmentary, and he was illiterate until he was taught to read and write by his wife, Eliza, whom he met and married in 1827, when he was nine-

teen. In the meantime, he had run away from the
cruel Raleigh tailor to whom he had been apprenticed, and he had escaped to Greenville, Tennessee,
with a price on his head. He opened his own tailor
shop in Greenville, and after he married seventeen-
year-old Eliza McArdle, a Greenville girl, he and
his new bride lived in one room at the rear of the
shop. Because of the extreme poverty of his early
years (his father died of overwork when young
Andrew was only three years old), he brought
with him to Tennessee a violent antipathy to supe-
riority of birth and wealth.

These firebrand ideas became known in Greenville, and young Johnson's tailor shop soon developed into the meeting place of all of the young
working-class political thinkers in the town, whose
idol was another self-made man of the people, the
then-President of the United States and national
war hero, Andrew Jackson. Every evening, more
and more of the idealistic young artisans and me-
chanics gathered in the tailor shop to discuss the
affairs of the nation, and in less than two years
Johnson had quite a political organization behind

him. Before he was twenty-one, there was enough of a vote among the tailor-shop philosophers to get him appointed an alderman of Greenville. Within a year he was mayor of the town.

After that, Johnson continued both to run his tailor shop and to run for public office. He was an imposing-looking man with tremendously broad shoulders, a shock of thick dark hair, sparkling black eyes, and ruggedly handsome features. His voice was mellow and pleasing, and as a biographer of the day noted, "It seems to entwine itself around the hearts of his followers and holds them spellbound, making him an effective stump-speaker." However, as he rose higher and higher in politics —from state legislator to Congressman to Governor of Tennessee to United States Senator—Johnson never rid himself of one flaw of personality which grated on his colleagues. He was constantly sensitive and defensive about his lack of polish and education and never ceased to remind all who would listen about his working-class origin.

Johnson was serving his first term in the Senate in April, 1862, when the Civil War broke out.

Wood engraving from *Frank Leslie's Illustrated Newspaper*, 1865   Courtesy Library of Congr

ANDREW JOHNSON TAKING THE OATH OF OFFICE

He had long had problems with his fellow Southern Democrats, voting independently on bills rather than following the party line, and becoming a champion of the small white farmer rather than the big slave-owner. In June, 1861, Tennessee seceded from the Union, and all the other members of the Tennessee delegation in Congress went home to join the Confederacy. Johnson, however, stubbornly remained alone in Washington and kept his seat in the Senate, working long and hard for peace, understanding, and the maintenance of the Union. When Tennessee was conquered by Union troops in 1862, President Lincoln appointed him the military governor of the state.

By making his solitary decision to remain loyal to the United States in the face of bitter public disapproval among his own friends and neighbors, the tough little tailor from the hills of Tennessee showed more valor and dedication to his own principles than he had ever exhibited before in his long and rather pedestrian political career.

But, says President Kennedy, fate caused the Republican Party to select Johnson as President

Lincoln's Vice-Presidential running mate in 1864. Within a few months an assassin's bullet thrust him into a position where his courage destroyed him but held back a dangerous tide that might have destroyed the country.

Profile Number 4

ANDREW JOHNSON
REFUSES TO PANIC

In the minds of most Americans, the primary fact about Andrew Johnson is that he was the only President ever to be impeached and the man who, in his trial by the Senate, came within one vote of being convicted of "high crimes and misdemeanors." His administration was an undistinguished one and consisted mainly of fighting losing battles with the same extremists in Congress who so nearly succeeded in unjustly removing him from office. And yet, in a way, Johnson exhibited as much courage after assuming the Presidency as many of those who preceded and followed him.

Johnson became President when Abraham Lincoln was assassinated on April 14, 1865, just five days after Lee surrendered to Grant at Appomattox. He walked directly into a host of troubles because he was the nominal head of a party of which he was actually not a member.

A Southern Democrat who had remained loyal to the Union, he had been selected as Lincoln's Vice-Presidential running mate in 1864 to emphasize that the Republican Party was for national unity. But when he actually became President, the so-called radical Republicans, bent on unrelenting revenge against the South, regarded him as an enemy.

A few weeks after he took office, Johnson courageously determined to pursue Lincoln's policy toward the defeated Confederacy, that is, regarding the Southern states as never having been out of the Union. He proceeded to appoint provisional governors for the former states of the Confederacy, leading to state constitutional conventions and elections of new state governments that would be cleansed of any active rebel elements.

As soon as Congress met, however, Johnson found himself in head-on conflict with Congressional leaders like Thaddeus Stevens and Charles Sumner, who considered the Southern states to be conquered provinces and wanted them treated as such. Johnson stubbornly stuck to his guns, but he was crushed by the Congressional steam roller which imposed harsh military governments on the South, overriding one Presidential veto after another.

Stevens, on the floor of Congress, called Johnson an "alien enemy, a citizen of a foreign state," and Sumner referred to the President as "an insolent drunken brute in comparison with which Caligula's horse was respectable."

This tragic conflict, which began in the first months of his administration, continued until its very end, and the Johnson era is generally considered one of the sorriest in American history. However, all but forgotten in those first few months was an unusual act of courage by Johnson for which we should all give thanks now, nearly one hundred years later.

TOP: PRESIDENT JOHNSON'S OFFICE UPSTAIRS
IN THE WHITE HOUSE

BOTTOM: THE OVAL ROOM IN THE WHITE HOUSE,
USED AS A LIBRARY UNDER THE JOHNSONS

Harper's Weekly Yearbook, 18

CARTOON PORTRAYING JOHNSON AS A CAESAR
IN HIS TREATMENT OF THE SOUTH

It might almost be considered an act of *reverse*
courage. It came about because, while the United
States was engaged in the Civil War, the French
Emperor, Napoleon III, took advantage of the
situation and established an enclave on the con-
tinent of North America. A French army invaded
Mexico in 1863, captured Mexico City, and in-
stalled Maximilian of Austria as emperor.

As soon as the War Between the States ended,
General Ulysses S. Grant and other military leaders—feeling their oats after their hard-won victory
over the South—demanded that an American
military expedition be sent to Mexico immediately
to smash the French-sponsored empire.

In the face of these demands by the country's
most popular war heroes, Johnson exhibited great
valor and held firm. He knew that his country,
bled white by the Civil War, was in no position to
tangle with the greatest land power in Europe, but
he stood up to Napoleon with courageous diplo-
macy. Through his Secretary of State, William
Seward, he continued to send strong notes to Paris.
One of these read, "The sympathies of the Amer-

PRESIDENT JOHNSON AND THE CARPETBAGGERS (1866)

ican people for the Republic of Mexico are very lively, and they are disposed to regard with impatience the continued intervention of France in that country."

Finally, in January, 1866, just nine months after Johnson took office, the French agreed to leave. In 1867, Maximilian was captured by the Mexican Army and executed. And so this most lightly regarded of Presidents was able to accomplish what none of his more illustrious predecessors had been able to do. By holding off his own hotheaded associates and by standing up to one of the greatest powers in the world, he affirmed the Monroe Doctrine once and for all.

V

The Spoilsman

Even more surprising than his choice of Andrew Johnson is President Kennedy's naming of the relatively unknown Chester A. Arthur as the fifth of his six brave Presidents. But, as Mr. Kennedy points out, valor among Presidents and Senators is much like valor on the battlefield. You never know in whom it is going to show up, and it is not limited to the brilliant and the illustrious.

There was little evidence of moral or political courage in tall, handsome Chester Alan Arthur during the fifty-one years which preceded his moving

into the White House. He was a distinguished-looking man, with dark hair and soulful brown eyes. With his flowing side-whiskers and full mustache, he might have passed for one of the matinee idols in the New York theater of his day. His life generally had been an easy one, and he drifted along, without protest, on the tides of corruption which typified American politics in the post-Civil War, get-rich-quick period. He was a wealthy New York City lawyer and machine politician, married to Ellen Lewis Heiden, the daughter of a famous explorer, and he was part of New York's high society in the heyday of the Vanderbilts and the Astors.

He was born in 1830 in Fairfield, Vermont, the eldest son of a well-to-do Baptist minister. His father, William Arthur, also was the author of a book on family names, still regarded as one of the curiosities of English literature. The eldest Arthur was a strange, willful man who insisted on personally educating his son until the latter was nine. Then the youngster entered the public schools and proved so bright that he was admitted to

from a photograph taken in 1880

THE BIRTHPLACE OF CHESTER A. ARTHUR, FAIRFIELD, VERMONT

Wood engraving from *Frank Leslie's Illustrated Newspaper,* 18

CHESTER A. ARTHUR TAKING OATH OF OFFICE

Union College in Schenectady, New York, when he was only fifteen. He graduated at eighteen, became the principal of a private school in Vermont, and then went on to study law. He was admitted to the bar in New York City at the age of twenty-two and immediately opened his own law office, which, from the very beginning, was quite a successful one.

Perhaps the main reason for its success was that young Arthur looked around, noted that there was opportunity for an up-and-coming lawyer in the newly emerging Republican Party (he had been a Whig), and promptly joined it. He was a delegate to the New York State Republicans' founding convention in Saratoga and soon became one of the key figures in a Republican political machine which managed to outdo the Democratic Tammany machine in the dispensing of jobs and favors to the faithful. Through the machine, Arthur was appointed Quartermaster General of New York State during the Civil War, and, according to the custom of the day, he handed out contracts freely to Republican campaign contributors. He also was in a good position to distribute largess when he became counsel to the New York City Board of Tax Commissioners.

But the handouts reached their peak in 1869, when Grant became President. Grant's administration was ridden with corruption, and the "King of Patronage" (paying off party stalwarts with an excessive number of political jobs) was Arthur's leader, Roscoe Conkling, by then a United States Senator. Conkling got President Grant to appoint Arthur to the job of collector of the port of New York. Under Arthur, the Custom House in New York City became so overstaffed with Republican political hacks who did little to earn their wages that the next Republican President, Rutherford B. Hayes, removed Arthur from office and ordered an investigation of the scandal.

And that was the sum total of Chester A. Arthur's inglorious political career, until fate—as it so often has done—thrust him unexpectedly into a position where it tapped some inner wellspring of strength and valor which never seemed to have existed before.

Profile Number 5

CHESTER A. ARTHUR
DEFIES THE BOSSES

There was courage of a different sort in the initial stages of the administration of another of our more obscure Presidents, whose tenure of office is generally regarded as a zero by the historians. President Kennedy calls Chester A. Arthur's courage the inner valor of a man who turned his back on his own past and his own personal supporters and reversed the attitude of a lifetime to do what he thought was right.

Arthur became President on September 19, 1881. He had been elected Vice-President the preceding November as part of a political deal that put James A. Garfield in the White House. Garfield was shot by a disappointed patronage-seeker, and Arthur ascended to the Presidency.

Arthur's elevation caused great exultation among the champions of political patronage. He had been

Cartoon by Thomas Nast   *Harper's Weekly Yearbook*, 188

OUT-"SHINING" EVERYBODY IN HUMILIATION AT ALBANY

New York: "I did not engage you, Vice-President
Arthur, to do this kind of work."

one of the most profligate dispensers of fat government jobs in his capacity as payoff man for the
powerful New York Republican political machine
headed by Senator Roscoe Conkling. It was to get
Conkling's support for dark-horse candidate Garfield that the Republican Convention of 1880 gave
the Vice-Presidential nomination to Conkling's
chief henchman, Arthur. Arthur's administration
therefore was expected to be one of the most corrupt in history.

But the Presidency does strange things to a man.
The moment he took office, the handsome, affable,
New York lawyer showed his independence of
Conkling and declared that the White House was
not going to be a fountainhead of corruption and
patronage payoffs, as the New York Custom
House had been under his aegis. He took this brave
step in the full knowledge that it would doom
him politically, as it did.

So Chester A. Arthur, the former patronage dispenser, severed his connection with the worst of
the spoilsmen, vetoed a graft-filled river and harbor
bill, and vigorously prosecuted spoilsmen who
were defrauding the Post Office.

Harper's Weekly Yearbook,

CARICATURE OF CHESTER A. ARTHUR (BY THOMAS NAST)

But, most noteworthy of all, the former patronage dispenser almost immediately began to press for a respectable Civil Service, in which government employees would be appointed according to competitive examinations instead of party loyalty, in which they would be promoted by merit alone, in which they could not be removed when the administration changed hands, and in which they would not spend their time and energy in political activity.

The result was the Pendleton Civil Service Act, the basis of our governmental employment policies to this day.

As he expected, Arthur was denied renomination by the angry leaders of his party in 1884, and he faded into obscurity. But the one act of courage of this all-but-forgotten man has remained a beacon for every President who has followed him.

VI

The Rough Rider

It is interesting that of the first five of the six brave Presidents chosen by President Kennedy, none, with the possible exception of John Quincy Adams, had a background or career similar to his own. With his last choice, Theodore Roosevelt, there are some interesting parallels. Both came from wealthy, distinguished families; both were war heroes; both were writers of best-selling books; both became President of the United States when very young. In fact, Roosevelt, at forty-two, was the youngest President we have ever had, and

AT EIGHTEEN

AT
FOUR YEARS

AT TEN
TO
TWELVE

AT TWENTY-THREE

THEODORE ROOSEVELT AT AGES 4, 10–12, 18, 23

Kennedy was just a few months older when he was inaugurated.

Roosevelt was the descendant, on his father's side, of a patrician Dutch family which settled in New York in the 1640's, and which also produced his distant cousin, President Franklin Delano Roosevelt. His mother was one of the aristocratic Bullochs of Georgia, and two of her brothers fought with great valor in the Confederate Navy during the Civil War.

Young Roosevelt was born in 1858 in his family's New York City mansion. He was a sickly child, suffering from asthma from the time he was an infant. As he wrote of himself, "I was a rather timid little boy, very fond of desultory reading and of natural history, and not excelling in any sport. Owing to my asthma I was not able to go to school, and I was nervous and self-conscious, so that as far as I can remember I was rather below than above my average playmate in point of leadership."

His schooling was all by private tutor. When he reached adolescence, however, his father put him on a stringent physical training program in order to build his body so he could enter Harvard College. As a result of his daily workouts in the gymnasium, young Roosevelt became amazingly strong and healthy, and he got into Harvard without any difficulty whatever. He remained a physical-culture faddist for the rest of his life.

He graduated from Harvard near the top of his class, and studied law briefly, but gave it up because he felt that it was devoted, not to justice, but "to getting people off." Finally, at twenty-four, he published a book, *The Naval War of 1812*, which was well received by the critics as "a work of considerable power." He was still restlessly searching for something to occupy him, however, and one day he joined his local Republican Club. Suddenly he had a meaningful area into which he could channel all his vast energies. Politics became his main interest from then on. He ran for the state Assembly and served three terms in the legislature, and—after a two-year hiatus as a cattle rancher in the Dakotas, during which he wrote three more books—he became a member of the Civil Service Commission, then Police Commissioner of New York, and then Assistant Secretary of the Navy. In each of these posts he developed a reputation as a fearless reformer. He tangled with the Republican Party bosses over graft and corruption, and his personal credo, as he himself stated it, was "When my duty is to enforce a law, that law is surely going to be enforced, without fear or favor. I am perfectly willing to be turned out—or be legislated out—but while in I mean business."

When the Spanish-American War began in 1898, Roosevelt resigned as Assistant Secretary of the Navy and became the colonel commanding the famous Rough Riders cavalry regiment. He returned with such a reputation as a national war hero that almost immediately he was elected governor of New York. He had a difficult time during his term as governor because his credo of enforcing the law without fear or favor was in fairly constant conflict with the less-rigid credo of New York Republican political boss Thomas C. Platt. Roosevelt was a good governor. He battled corruption, instituted important administrative reforms, and pushed through a bill which banned race discrimination in the New York schools. He

COLONEL THEODORE ROOSEVELT OF THE ROUGH RIDERS

infuriated his industry-backed party, however, with bills such as one which enforced a tax on corporations.

By 1900, the Republican political machine was ready to do anything to get rid of Roosevelt. He was too popular with the people to eliminate him by ordinary methods, so an elaborate plan was conceived to kick him upstairs into the Vice-Presidency of the United States, under President William McKinley, and thus render him harmless.

But like many such carefully laid plans, the scheme went awry. A few months after Roosevelt took office, McKinley was assassinated—and, as President Kennedy points out, the scene was set for an already courageous man to prove himself once again under fire.

Profile Number 6

THEODORE ROOSEVELT BACKS A REVOLT

We all know about the courage of Theodore

Roosevelt as exemplified by his big-game expeditions to Africa and his charge up San Juan Hill at the head of his Rough Riders in the Spanish-American War. His first few months in office after he succeeded the assassinated President McKinley served to confirm that reputation.

His party had hoped to bury him in the Vice-Presidency, but when he took office as President, one of his first actions was to proceed to break up the big business trusts—powerful interests that had openly defied the Sherman Anti-Trust Act. Since Roosevelt's standing with the leaders of his party was already shaky, this action seemed certain to doom any chance he might have for renomination and reelection in 1904, but he took his crusade to the people and won.

From the very beginning of his administration, Roosevelt was determined to build the Panama Canal. With new American possessions in both the Caribbean and the Pacific, he felt it was absolutely essential to our defense to have the short-cut waterway for the rapid maneuvering of the American Navy. He began to negotiate with the Repub-

Harper's Weekly Yearbook, Vol. II, 1905

PRESIDENT THEODORE ROOSEVELT "BOWLING" AT GRAFT AND CORRUPTION

Underwood & Underwood

"WHEN THE PRESIDENT MAKES A SPEECH"

lic of Colombia, which then owned Panama, to lease a six-mile-wide strip of land across the Isthmus of Panama. When Colombia became recalcitrant, Roosevelt played a part in an event which had a lasting effect on American history.

On November 3, 1903, while three American warships stood off the Isthmus of Panama, a revolution broke out in Panama City. The revolutionary army consisted of the city's fire brigade and three hundred section hands from the Panama railroad. The insurrection was bloodless, and the next day Dr. Manuel Amada, soon to be President of Panama, read a declaration of independence and declared the new Republic of Panama. Two weeks later, Panama concluded a treaty leasing the Canal Zone to the United States in perpetuity.

Did it take courage for Roosevelt to make the decisions required in this delicate situation? It most certainly did. As he wrote to his son shortly after the Panama revolution, "My experience in these matters gives me an idea of the fearful times Lincoln must have had in the great crisis he had to face."

Epilogue

Illumination Through the Window

As historian Theodore H. White points out, President Kennedy, in making these choices of six brave Presidents, has opened a window on himself. Says White, the author of the highly acclaimed *The Making of the President—1960*, "The President seems to be fascinated above all by a common quality in these predecessors of his—by their ability to make solitary decisions, by their courage in cutting across public disapproval, by their clear perception of what must be done in time of confusion. In the problems of these men and the solutions they found, one sees reflected clearly the problems and the alternatives, and the hopes and fears that must perplex President Kennedy's thinking, too."

This seemed to me to be true in all my discussions with the President. We also talked about more recent, better known acts of Presidential heroism which fell into the same category: Franklin D. Roosevelt's First Hundred Days, in which he instituted dozens of dramatic new measures to help conquer the blackest economic depression the country had ever faced; Harry Truman's soul-searching in deciding to drop the first atomic bomb on Hiroshima, to bring the unprecedented bloodshed of World War II to a more speedy end; Dwight D. Eisenhower's first efforts to end the Korean War.

But like all historians, President Kennedy seems to like to probe more obscure areas of our American heritage for lessons that can be put to use today. His fertile mind kept darting back to the Presidents few of us remember—the John Tylers, the James K. Polks. As we finished our talk, he said, "History not only teaches, it illuminates. And with illumination, we can penetrate the darkness of any problem that threatens us in the months and years that lie ahead."

Set in Janson
Format by Jean Krulis
Manufactured by Murray Printing Co. and The Haddon Craftsmen, Inc.
Published by Harper & Row, Publishers